by Libby Romero

Table of Contents

Introduction 2
Chapter 1 What Are Comets? 4
Chapter 2 What Parts Do Comets Have? 8
Chapter 3 Who Learned About Comets? 12
Conclusion 18
Concept Map 20
Glossary 22
Index 24

Introduction

Comets are bright objects in space. Comets are balls of burning gas.

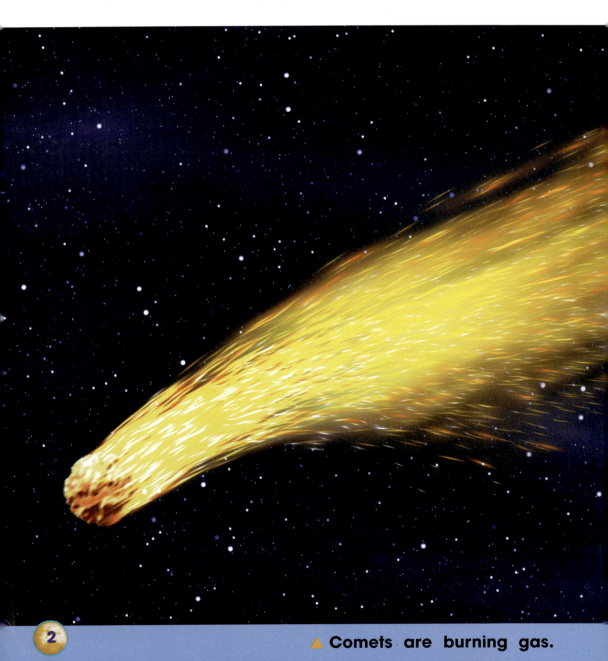

▲ **Comets are burning gas.**

Words to Know

astronomers

coma

comets

nucleus

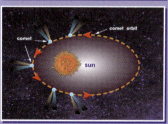
orbit

universe

See the Glossary on page 22.

Chapter 1

What Are Comets?

Comets are in the **universe**.

▲ Comets move in the universe.

Comets are in **orbit**.

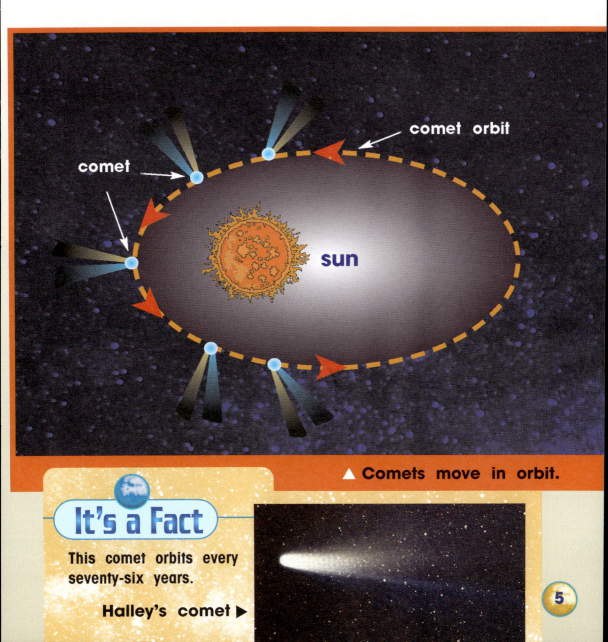

▲ Comets move in orbit.

It's a Fact

This comet orbits every seventy-six years.

Halley's comet ▶

Chapter 1

Comets are dust.

▲ Comets have dust.

Comets are gases.

▲ Comets have gases.

What Are Comets?

Comets are ice.

▲ Comets have ice.

Chapter 2

What Parts Do Comets Have?

Comets have three parts.

▲ This comet has three parts.

Comets have a **nucleus**.

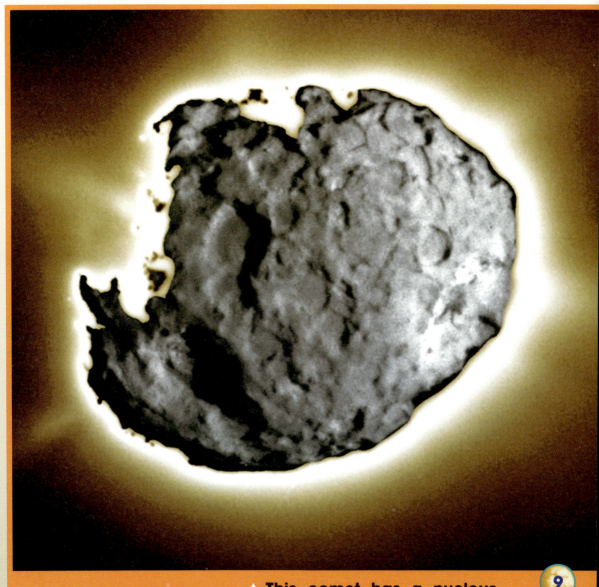

▲ This comet has a nucleus.

Chapter 2

Comets have a **coma**.

It's a Fact
Some comas are very big.

▲ This comet has a coma.

What Parts Do Comets Have?

Comets have tails.

▲ This comet has a long tail.

Chapter 3

Who Learned About Comets?

Astronomers learned about comets.

▲ Astronomers studied comets.

Scientists learned about comets.

Did You Know?
Scientists are people who study science.

▲ Scientists studied comets.

Chapter 3

Tycho Brahe learned about comets.

▲ **Tycho Brahe studied comets.**

Who Learned About Comets?

Sir Isaac Newton learned about comets.

▲ Sir Isaac Newton studied comets.

Chapter 3

Edmond Halley learned about comets.

▲ **Edmond Halley studied comets.**

Who Learned About Comets?

People learned about comets.

▲ People studied comets.

It's a Fact

People use telescopes to study comets.

▲ People use this telescope.

Conclusion

Comets are part of the universe.

Concept Map

Comets

What Are Comets?

- in the universe
- in orbit
- dust
- gases
- ice

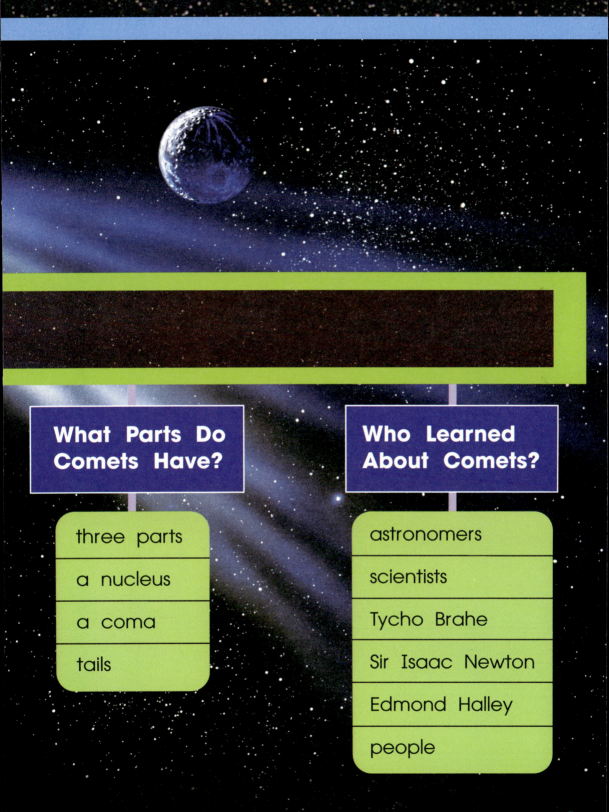

What Parts Do Comets Have?

- three parts
- a nucleus
- a coma
- tails

Who Learned About Comets?

- astronomers
- scientists
- Tycho Brahe
- Sir Isaac Newton
- Edmond Halley
- people

Glossary

astronomers people who study the universe

Astronomers learned about comets.

coma dust and gases around the nucleus

Comets have a coma.

comets bright objects in space

Comets have three parts.

nucleus the middle of an object

Comets have a nucleus.

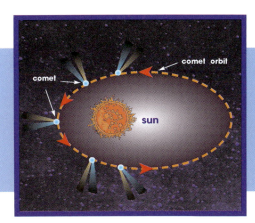

orbit the path followed while circling another object

*Comets are in **orbit**.*

universe everything in space

*Comets are in the **universe**.*

Index

astronomers, 12

Brahe, Tycho, 14

coma, 10

comets, 3, 4–18

dust, 6

gas, 2, 6

Halley, Edmond, 16

ice, 7

Newton, Sir Isaac, 15

nucleus, 9

orbit, 5

parts, 8

tails, 11

universe, 4, 18